Poems for God

Moselle Slaten Blackwell

By God's grace and the Holy Spirit, I have tried to capture the beauty of the scriptures in each of these poems.

There may be those who don't read the Bible; hopefully these poems will inspire interest in studying the scriptures.

MSB

TEACH Services, Inc.
PUBLISHING
www.TEACHServices.com ● (800) 367-1844

Copyright © 2016, 2019 Moselle Slaten Blackwell
Copyright © 2019 TEACH Services, Inc.
ISBN-13: 978-1-4796-0767-9 (Paperback)
ISBN-13: 978-1-4796-0825-6 (ePub)

Scripture quotations marked The Message are taken from The Message. Copyright © 1993, 1994, 1995, 1996, 2000, 2001, 2002. Used by permission of NavPress Publishing Group.

Scripture quotations marked NASB are taken from the New American Standard Bible®, copyright © 1960, 1962, 1963, 1968, 1971, 1972, 1973, 1975, 1977, 1995 by The Lockman Foundation. Used by permission.

Scripture quotations marked NIV are taken from The Holy Bible, New International Version®, NIV®. Copyright © 1973, 1978, 1984, 2011 by Biblica, Inc.™ Used by permission All rights reserved worldwide.

Texts credited to NKJV are taken from the New King James Version®. Copyright © 1982 by Thomas Nelson, Inc. Used by permission. All rights reserved.

Scripture quotations marked NLT are taken from the Holy Bible, New Living Translation, copyright © 1996, 2004, 2007 by Tyndale House Foundation. Used by permission of Tyndale House Publishers, Inc., Carol Stream, Illinois 60188. All rights reserved.

Scripture quotations marked REB are taken from The Revised English Bible, copyright © Cambridge University Press and Oxford University Press 1989. All rights reserved.

TEACH Services, Inc.
P U B L I S H I N G
www.TEACHServices.com • (800) 367-1844

Special Acknowledgment

I wish to acknowledge and thank my daughter, Charlotte for her expertise in submitting the needed information on the computer for me.

Table of Contents

I Love You Lord

Genesis 12

I love Your beautiful sunsets and Your moonlight nights.
They testify of Your majesty and might.

The mighty seas and evergreen trees are evidence of Your love;
The rains in spring and the winter snow, You send from above.

I love You for the strength You give each day to start anew.
I love You for my eyes to see the lovely things You do.

I love You for the flowers that bloom, when summer comes around;
Even for the pinecones, from the evergreen that fall to the ground.

You are so mighty and so strong, as only You can be.
Help me to love You more, and everyone, because You first loved me.

Jesus Christ: God With Us

Hebrews 1:8; Luke 1:35; Matthew 1:23; John 1:1–3

Why can't people understand that Jesus Christ is God-Man?

He is God the Son, second of the Godhead. Equal to the Father, Philippians 2:6 has said.

Jesus Christ, from eternity past, the carnal mind cannot grasp.

Born of a virgin, God did tell; call My Son Emmanuel.

Deity and humanity, inseparably bound. The secret of this mystery in God only is found.

The Son of God took the form of humanity, to identify with you and me.

Jesus is fully God and fully Man;

Only through faith do we accept what we cannot understand.

This Man who walked the earthly sod, was Jesus Christ, the Son of God.

God's Requirements

Micah 6:8

To do justly and have mercy is what we must do.

God requires this from me and from you.

To walk humbly is also God's command.

Jesus Christ will lead us, for He is our Friend.

Incline Our Hearts

I Kings 8:58

Please Lord, to You I sincerely pray;
Give me the words I should speak today.

Your love, grace, and judgments are pure.
For those who follow Your will, eternity is sure.

Incline our hearts to praise You for Your blessings and grace.
May we all be ready, when You come, to leave this place.

Tomorrow may not come for me;
If this be so, save my soul, I plea.

Our Only Redeemer

Isaiah 43:1–2

I have created and redeemed you and called you by name.

Fear not and hold fast.

Yesterday, today, and forever,

I am the same.

Take no thought for tomorrow,

Think not of the past.

When you pass through the fires of life and the waters of time,

I will be with you; you are Mine.

The Last Temptation

Luke 22:39–42

With His disciples, Christ slowly walked to Gethsemane;
Heart full of sorrow in contemplation of His last agony.

He had visited this place many times for meditation and prayer,
Now longing for His disciples to pray with Him there.

The sins of men weighed so heavily on Him,
He fell to His knees; all strength had left Him.

Under divine Justice He suffered;
For my sins and yours, Himself He offered.

The conflict was terrible; Satan tempted Him so;
Not to give His life for this world of woe.

Go back to Your Father and His throne on high;
Why save those who hate You? Why will You die?

Jesus prayed three times His bitter cup to pass;
Not My will, O God, but Thine, was His final plea, at last.

By constant prayer to God His Father, Jesus was able to overcome;
The greatest temptation of Satan He has forever won.

Satan knew when Jesus died that day on Calvary,
His destiny was surely sealed throughout eternity.

Faith

Hebrews 11:1–6, 30–33

Without faith, we cannot please God,
For faith is the key;
The substance of things hoped for
And proof of things we cannot see.

By faith we turn to God in prayer.
In faith we understand,
The worlds were framed by the Word of God
And sustained by His hand.

By faith, Abel gained a good report,
For the sacrifice he made.
God testified of his gift,
And mercy on him laid.

By faith David subdued kingdoms.
Rahab perished not—
Barak, Gideon, and Joshua will never be forgot.

By faith, when Abraham was tried,
He offered up his son.
Because of his obedience,
God's favor he has won.

By faith we live for You, O Lord;
Don't let our lights grow dim.
By faith we know God will return,
To take the faithful home with Him.

Pilate: The Governor

Matthew 27:11–31

Jesus was taken before Pilate
Who found no fault in Him.
Then sent to Herod,
Who sent Him to Pilate again.

Pilate's wife informed him of a dream
She had one night.
"Have nothing to do with that just Man,
For He is God's Delight."

Pilate perceived who Jesus was;
His life he tried to save.
But because of his position and fear,
Jesus went to His prophetic grave.

Pilate decided what no one else could decide;
He washed his hands and sentenced Jesus to be crucified.

Judas Iscariot: The Betrayal

Matthew 26:47–50

Jesus told His disciples that He would be betrayed
By one of them for whom He had often prayed.

Judas betrayed his Lord for thirty pieces of silver;
They promised this to Judas, if Christ he would deliver.

Judas greeted Jesus with a kiss as he entered Gethsemane.
Jesus was arrested, without a word, to meet His destiny.

When Judas saw that Jesus Christ resisted not His fate,
He threw the silver to the ground—
But then, it was too late.

Prayer for Victory

I John 5:4

I prayed for victory over my sin.
God heard my prayer and strengthened me to win.

I pray His will be done in my life,
To give me peace in the midst of strife.

I don't know from day to day what God has planned for me,
But I will pray for Him to lead; He gives the victory.

Exalt the Lord

Psalm 46:10

Exalt Me, My people, among the heathen,
Exalt Me in all the earth.
I am the Sovereign of the universe,
Your Creator and your worth.

Rejoice and sing praises
For God's mercies from above.
Be still, be reverent and know,
God is love.

You Can

Philippians 4:13

In prayer seek God's guidance in all you do.
He will never fail; He will see you through.
He is your success.
What you do, He will bless.

If ever discouraged when failures come,
Do not give up—you have just begun.
Go step-by-step when you start;
Be determined in your heart.

To pursue life eternal should be our ultimate goal.
Stand firm in Jesus; give Him your soul.
Never make a plan without God's command;
Have faith to believe you can—
You CAN.

God's New Creation

John 14:1–3; Revelation 21:1–5

Don't let your heart be troubled, my friend.
Jesus has promised He is coming again.

He died on the cross our sins to forgive.
He is coming to make the world a new place to live.

He promised mansions to those who believe.
Do not doubt His promise and your gift you will receive.

No more tears, pain, death, or sorrow;
Nothing bad to mar tomorrow.

There will be no more sin or sea;
The world will be pure and perfect throughout eternity.

The Light of Jesus

II Corinthians 4:6

God spoke the light into existence by a single command.

His words brought forth light, when darkness covered the land.

To save us from the darkness of sin,

He sent His Son of righteousness, to us, to dwell within.

The knowledge of God sent from above to shine within each heart,

Is the light of Jesus Christ the very Son of God.

Share

Galatians 6:9, 10

How can we not think of others when God thinks of us?
He gives us everything we need—can we but share the same?

We must not be weary in our services for God.
We are called to do His work: to lift up Jesus' name.

Do not put off for tomorrow what we can do today.
As we have opportunity, let's hasten to obey.

We may not have a lot, but we can share what we've got.
And in due season we shall reap, if we share and faint not.

Our Priest and King

Hebrews 2:17, 18

Jesus left His throne on high,
Descended to the earth.
He became a human
Through His humble birth.

There was no other way,
No other way, it seems.
So God sent His only Son,
For sinners to redeem.

He was tempted as we are
And suffered everything:
Desertion, hatred, and ridicule,
For salvation to us bring.

He came, He lived, He bled and died,
And then He rose again;
Ascended to His throne on high,
To be our Priest and King.

Job: The Challenge

Job 38

Job had pain and lost everything he had,
But he never doubted God, though he was very sad.

In his affliction he asked "Why?"
And this is God's infinite reply:

"Where were you when I created the worlds?
When I shut up the sea with doors, to control when it roars?

Can you bind the seven stars of Pleiades?
Or hold Orion in his place?

Can you bring forth Mazzaroth in his season?
Or can you guide Arcturus? Give Me a reason!

I am God—you are man.
Answer Me, if you can!"

Job confessed.
God blessed:

"Job, please, do not despair.
I love you and I really care."

Strength To Live

Romans 6:2–4

When tempted, O God, to stray from Your side,
Be our keeper, be our guide.

How can we, who are dead to sin,
Live any longer therein?

Give us strength, Lord, all day long;
We are weak, but You are strong.

Let our thoughts be pure and right.
Keep us ever by Your might.

Keep us humble; hold us fast.
Please take us home with You at last.

Og: King of Bashan

Deuteronomy 3:1–25

Og, King of Bashan, had much power in his hand.
A remnant of the Rephaim,
His enemies, many, feared him.

His bedstead of iron was thirteen feet long and six feet wide;
Exhibited in Rabbath-Ammon—
The ancients' pride.

His conquered territory extended from the river Jabbock to Mount Hermon.
It was given to Moses and the Israelites,
As was Heshbon.

God is greater than any man;
Even Og, the giant,
The King of Bashan.

David: King of Israel

I Samuel 16:1–12; I Samuel 24:1–8

God chose David to be King of Israel.
Saul was displeased, but his anger he withheld.

Saul sought to take David's life many times.
But to take Saul's life was not in David's mind.

One day Saul went into a cave.
David cut off his skirt, but Saul's life he saved.

David honored Saul as God's anointed.
He dared not take the life of God's appointed.

David was a warrior from the start.
He was also a man "after God's own heart."

David sinned, it is true.
He repented, and God forgave him, as He forgives me and you.

David could not build God's temple because of the blood on his hand.
But Solomon, his son, was chosen to build
the most magnificent temple in the land.

Solomon: King of Israel

I Kings 3:4–15; II Chronicles 6:12–42

A man of peace in the sight of God:
That's what his name means.
He was the wisest man who lived,
And the richest man it seems.

Solomon walked upright before the Lord,
His will he obeyed.
He did not ask for riches,
But for wisdom he prayed.

Because he prayed for wisdom,
God gave him riches, too.
He used his wealth to help mankind,
As God knew he would do.

Solomon was chosen to build God's house.
So beautiful it stood;
Made of gold, silver, cedar, brass,
And precious acacia wood.

So famous was his wisdom
And his kingdom to behold,
The queen of Sheba said of him,
"The half has not been told."

Solomon dedicated the temple,
With a most solemn prayer;
For God to lead His people,
He had put in His care.

Solomon truly loved the Lord,
But he began to stray;
Away from his Maker,
His wives to obey.

He began to worship idols,
And strange things he did do.
He said it is all vanity;
A warning for me and you.

Martha, Martha

Luke 10:38–42

Jesus came to Martha's home by her gracious invitation.
Mary, Martha's sister, was concerned by another situation.

While Martha prepared the meal for them to eat,
Mary sat at Jesus' feet.
Mary was not doing what she could, Martha felt;
So she came to Jesus to petition Mary's help.

"Martha, Martha," Jesus said,
"You are concerned about many things, I am afraid.
Mary has chosen that good part,
Which shall not be taken away;
For she loves Me with a sincere heart."

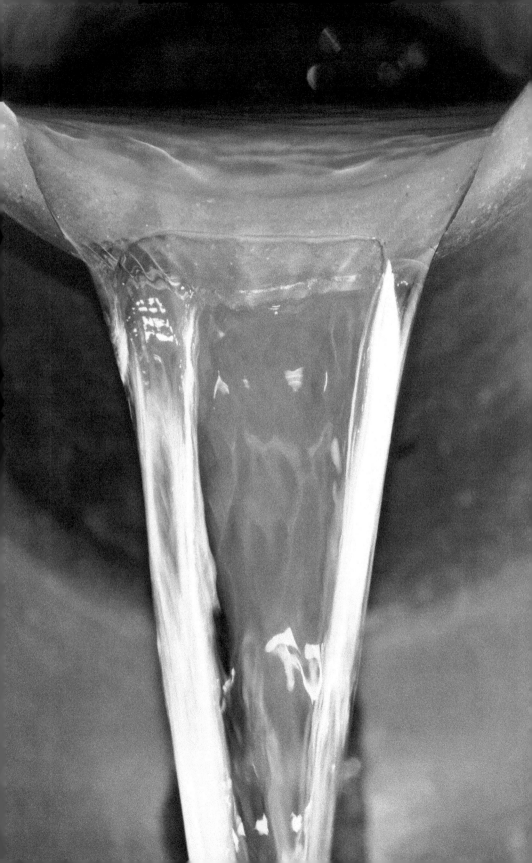

What Manner of Man?

John 2:1–10; John 21:25; Mark 4:41

Jesus walked on the sea so long ago.
Demanded the demons, of a possessed man, to go.

Jesus was sleeping when the disciples' boat was tossed vehemently;
He awoke and commanded, "Peace be still," to the wind and the sea.

Jesus healed a woman with a disease she had for twelve years,
On His way to raise a child, whose death had caused her family many tears.

Jesus cleansed a leper who sought Him earnestly;
Because the man believed, He healed him graciously.

Jesus had compassion on the multitudes He taught.
He fed them twice with bread and fish by the miracles He wrought.

The miracle of Cana, Jesus' turning water to wine,
Will always be remembered as His most gracious miracle, of all time.

John's account of Jesus' life and His work on earth,
Would take too many books to write of His eternal worth.

Samson

Judges 13–16

The angel of the Lord came to Manoah's barren wife,
To tell her of the son she would have in her life.

She was to drink no wine nor eat anything unclean;
Her son would be to God a holy Nazarene.

His head would not be shaven, not at any time.
He would deliver Israel from the Philistines.

When the child was born, they named him "Samson."
The child grew, and the Lord blessed him.

Samson fell in love with the daughter of a Philistine;
She gave away the answer to the riddle of his rhyme.

Samson's wife was given to another man.
This angered him so,
He burned a field of corn with jackals and firebrands.

The Philistines wanted to capture Samson but they knew
not the source of his strength;
They asked Delilah, whom he loved, to question him at length.

Delilah told the Philistines, Samson's hair is what made him strong.
They shaved his head, put out eyes, and made him labor long.

Samson was brought to entertain the Philistines one night.
He prayed for God to give him strength to avenge the loss of his sight.

He was brought to stand between two pillars in a place where
three-thousand people gathered.

He leaned upon the pillars with all his might.
Samson destroyed more Philistines in his death than he did in his life,
that night.

Mary: Mother of Jesus

Luke 1:26–38

In a city called Nazareth,
The Angel Gabriel visited a young virgin named Mary.
Gabriel told her she would conceive a son; "His name shall be called Jesus."
Of this news, Mary was not contrary.

Being a virgin, she questioned how this could be.
Gabriel said, "The Holy Ghost shall come upon you,
And the power of the Highest shall overshadow thee."

Mary was humble and obedient in her heart,
For she knew that Holy Thing which shall be born of her,
Shall be called the Son of God.

TEACH Services, Inc.
P U B L I S H I N G

We invite you to view the complete
selection of titles we publish at:
www.TEACHServices.com

We encourage you to write us
with your thoughts about this,
or any other book we publish at:
info@TEACHServices.com

TEACH Services' titles may be purchased in
bulk quantities for educational, fund-raising,
business, or promotional use.
bulksales@TEACHServices.com

Finally, if you are interested in seeing
your own book in print, please contact us at:
publishing@TEACHServices.com
We are happy to review your manuscript at no charge.

CPSIA information can be obtained
at www.ICGtesting.com
Printed in the USA
BVHW060746120719
553260BV00004B/60/P